student
toasties

STUDENT TOASTIES
TOASTIE HEAVEN FOR STUDENTS ON A BUDGET

ISBN 978-1-911219-00-2

A CIP catalogue record of this book is available from the British Library

DISCLAIMER

Some recipes may contain nuts or traces of nuts. Those suffering from any allergies associated with nuts should avoid any recipes containing nuts or nut based oils.

This information is provided and sold with the knowledge that the publisher and author do not offer any legal or other professional advice.

In the case of a need for any such expertise consult with the appropriate professional.

This book does not contain all information available on the subject, and other sources of recipes are available.

This book has not been created to be specific to any individual's requirements.

Every effort has been made to make this book as accurate as possible. However, there may be typographical and or content errors. Therefore, this book should serve only as a general guide and not as the ultimate source of subject information.

This book contains information that might be dated and is intended only to educate and entertain.

The author and publisher shall have no liability or responsibility to any person or entity regarding any loss or damage incurred, or alleged to have incurred, directly or indirectly, by the information contained in this book.

CONTENTS

TOASTIES FROM STUDENTS AROUND THE WORLD 49

GRILLED & OPEN TOASTIES 61

POSH TOASTIES 75

SWEET TOASTIES 83

INTRODUCTION

The Toastie Is King!

So you're a student! From studying to socialising you have many calls on your time and the chances are you have to take care of your own meals too – no easy thing when you're pushed for time and money. But fear not! We have the ideal solution for you: toasties!

Why? Because everyone loves toast! It's the ultimate comfort fare and, for some reason, sticking just about any other food between two slices of it makes crispy, golden, gooey perfection on a plate. In fact you don't even need a plate – eat on the go when you're in a rush.

Toasties are quick, easy, satisfying and cheap. They hit the spot, they're ridiculously tasty and they leave very little mess or washing up. Plus you can eat them for any meal. With the filling of your choice they're superb for breakfast, lunch, dinner or any snack in between. In the world of the student the supposedly humble toastie is king!

So get in there: beg or borrow a toastie maker from family or friends; or even invest in a new or second-hand one between flatmates. You won't regret it. But if you can't lay your hands on one, don't despair – most toasties can be done under the grill instead.

So long as you have bread of any kind, you can rustle up a delicious toasted sarnie out of just about anything. Make good use of leftovers from dinner the night before. Slap on fresh salad vegetables, inexpensive ham or chicken, tinned fish, cheese of any variety, and you have an instant, warming, tasty meal that you can eat on the go, or in a brief break in your schedule, sprawling on the sofa watching TV. Or even while you're studying!

In this easy recipe collection, you'll find toastie ideas for all tastes and occasions, all geared towards a student's life, health and pocket: a great choice of meat and fish fillings; vegetarian options; and sweet and gooey toasties for those moments when only sugar will do. There are even some posher recipes for when you have the urge for something more sophisticated. And for those who don't yet have a toastie machine, there's an open & grilled collection especially for toasting under the grill.

And talking of the toastie machine, since it's going to be working hard for you, you do need to look after it! But rejoice: it takes only a moment to wipe it down after use, so that neither the machine nor you nor the next toastie gets damaged by old bits of food.

Cleaning & Care Hints

• Always unplug the machine before cleaning.

• While the plates are still warm but not hot, wipe with damp kitchen towels or sponge to remove any grease.

• Use a non-metallic heat-proof spatula to remove more stubborn residue.

• Use a small sponge with warm soapy water to scrub the plates.

• Wipe dry with kitchen paper towels or a dry clean cloth.

• Never use any abrasive cleaning products or scourers on the plates of your machine. This will ruin the non-stick coating and make your toastie machine useless.

• Allow the plates to air dry before closing the lid.

• "Season" the plates to preserve the non-stick. To do this brush the plates lightly with sunflower oil, close the lid and heat to its highest setting for 5 minutes. It is a good idea to do this periodically to get the best out of your machine.

• Always read the manufactures guidelines for your appliance.

Toastie Tips

• Always heat up your machine before adding the bread. We recommend the highest setting.

• Use oven gloves. The plates obviously become very hot and you can easily burn your fingers if you're not careful.

• For each toastie, either brush your plates with oil, or butter the bread on the outside - the recipes tell you which is recommended in each case.

• Avoid using low fat spreads as these can result in your toastie sticking and burning.

• Try to leave a small gap around the edges of your sandwich so that ingredients don't spill out onto your machine.

• Don't overfill your sarnie. Though tempting, it will inevitably make a mess of your machine!

• When making a thicker toastie close the lid slowly, applying gradual pressure until it fully closes and/or clicks into place. Don't force the lid shut.

• Never cook raw meat or fish in your toastie maker!

Enjoy!

meat feast toasties

Classic Ham and Egg Toastie

Ingredients

- Vegetable or sunflower oil for brushing
- 1 egg
- 1½ tbsp Worcestershire sauce
- ½ tsp Tabasco sauce
- Salt and pepper to taste
- 2 slices bread
- 3 slices cooked ham
- 40g/1½oz Cheddar cheese

1 Brush your toastie maker with a little oil to help prevent sticking and make your toastie nice and crispy. Switch on and bring up to its highest temperature.

2 Meanwhile, whisk together the egg, Worcestershire sauce and Tabasco in a bowl. Season with salt and pepper, then pour the mixture into a wide, shallow dish. Soak the bread in the egg mixture.

3 Thinly slice or grate the cheese.

4 Place one slice of egg-soaked bread in the heated toastie maker. Layer the ham and cheese on top. Add the other slice of bread.

5 Close the lid tightly and leave to cook for 3-4 minutes or until the cheese melts and the toastie is crisp and golden.

Eggs are a great source of protein to give you long-lasting energy.

Turkey and Pesto Toastie

Ingredients

- Vegetable or sunflower oil for brushing
- 2 slices bread
- 2 tsp basil pesto
- 2 slices cheese
- 2 slices roast turkey

1 Brush your toastie maker with a little oil to help prevent sticking and make your toastie nice and crispy. Switch on and bring up to its highest temperature.

2 On one slice of bread, arrange a slice of turkey. Spread one teaspoon of pesto over it. Add the cheese, the rest of the pesto and the second slice of turkey.

3 Top with the remaining slice of bread and place your sandwich in the toastie maker.

4 Close the lid tightly and leave to cook for 3-4 minutes or until the cheese melts and the toastie is crisp and golden brown.

Serve with a tomato and green leafy salad.

Corned Beef Toastie

Ingredients

- 2 slices corned beef
- ¼ onion
- 25g/1oz Cheddar cheese
- 1 tsp mayonnaise

- ½ tsp mustard
- 1 tsp sweet pickle relish
- 2 slices bread
- A large knob of butter

1 Switch on your toastie maker and bring up to temperature.

2 Shred the corned beef into a bowl. Peel and chop a little onion and add it to the bowl. Grate about an ounce of cheese and add it to the bowl, along with the mayonnaise, mustard, pickle relish, and parsley flakes. Mix it all up.

3 Butter the bread and place one slice in the toastie maker butter side down. Spread the corned

beef mixture carefully over the bread. Add the top slice, butter side up.

4 Close the lid tightly and leave to cook for 3-4 minutes or until the toastie is crisp and golden brown.

Vary the amounts of mayonnaise, mustard and pickle to suit your own taste.

★ ★ ★ ★ ★ ★ ★ ★

Ham Mayonnaise Toastie

Ingredients

- Vegetable or sunflower oil for brushing
- 2 slices of bread
- 2 tsp mayonnaise
- 40g/1½oz cheese
- 1 slice ham
- 1 slice onion

1 Brush your toastie maker with a little oil to help prevent sticking and make your toastie nice and crispy. Switch on your toastie maker and bring up to temperature.

2 While it's heating, grate your cheese and roughly chop the slice of onion.

3 Spread mayonnaise over both slices of bread. Sprinkle half the cheese over one. Add the onion and the ham and then the rest of the cheese. Put the top on the sandwich and transfer to your toastie maker.

4 Close the lid tightly and leave to cook for 3-4 minutes or until the toastie is crisp and golden brown.

You can use any kind of cheese with this recipe so feel free to experiment with the flavours and quantity.

Chicken and Ham Toastie

Ingredients

- 2 slices of bread
- Knob of butter
- 1 tbsp soured cream

- 2 slices Gruyere cheese
- 1 slice cooked chicken breast
- 1 slice ham

1 Switch on your toastie maker and bring up to temperature.

2 Meanwhile, slice the cheese, chicken and ham as necessary. Butter one side of each slice of bread; spread soured cream on the other side.

3 Place one slice of bread, butter side down, in the toastie maker. Layer on one slice of cheese, chicken, ham, more cheese, and, finally the second slice of bread, butter side up.

4 Close the lid tightly and leave to cook for 3-4 minutes or until the cheese has melted and the toastie is crisp and golden brown.

This is a great way to liven up leftover chicken. If you don't have Gruyere cheese just use whatever is to hand.

Hawaiian Toastie

Ingredients

- 1 ring of tinned pineapple
- Knob of butter
- 2 slices of bread

- 2 slices cheese
- 2 slices cooked ham

1 Switch on your toastie maker and bring it up to temperature.

2 While it's heating, open a tin of pineapple and drain; chop one ring into small chunks. Cut 2 slices of cheese.

3 Butter the bread. Place one slice butter side down in your heated toastie maker. Layer on the cheese, ham, and chopped pineapple.

4 Place the remaining slices of bread on top with the butter side up. Close the lid tightly and leave to cook for 3-4 minutes or until the cheese has melted and the toastie is crisp and golden brown.

Pineapple is great for boosting your vitamin C and energy levels.

Bacon and Tomato Toastie

Ingredients

- 2 slices of bread
- 2 bacon rashers
- 1 tomato
- A few sprigs of flat leaf parsley
- Knob of butter
- Freshly ground black pepper

1 Grill the bacon and then roughly chop it.

2 Switch on the toastie maker. While it heats, wash and slice the tomato and chop the parsley.

3 Butter the bread and place the first slice in the toastie maker, butter side down. Arrange the bacon on the bread and sprinkle it with pepper. Place the tomato slices on top, then the parsley, and top with the second slice of bread, butter side up.

4 Close the lid tightly and toast until the sandwich is crisp and golden brown.

If you don't have parsley, substitute with a couple of lettuce leaves.

Pizza Toastie

Ingredients

- Knob of butter
- 2 slices of bread
- 4 thin slices mozzarella

- 6 slices pepperoni
- 1 spoonful tomato passata

1 Switch on the toastie maker. While it heats, cut your slices of mozzarella and pepperoni, and butter the bread.

2 Place one slice of bread in your toastie maker, butter side down. Layer on the mozzarella, pepperoni and a slathering of passata. Finish with the remaining slice of bread, butter side up.

3 Close the lid of your toastie maker tightly and toast until the cheese in melting and sandwich is crisp and golden brown.

Substitute ketchup for passata if you like.

Sausage, Cheese and Tomato Toastie

Ingredients

- 2 sausages
- 40g/1½oz cheese
- 1 tomato

- 2 slices of bread
- Knob of butter

1 Grill the sausages, then cut them in half length-wise.

2 Switch on the toastie maker. While it heats, grate the cheese, wash and slice the tomato.

3 Butter the bread and place the first slice in the toastie maker, butter side down. Arrange the sausages on the bread and sprinkle the cheese over them. Place the tomato slices on top, and cover with the second slice of bread, butter side up.

4 Close the lid tightly and cook until the cheese is melted and the toastie is crisp and golden brown.

If you prefer the Scottish version 1 or 2 slices of square sausage will work just as well.

Roast Beef and Onion Toastie

Ingredients

- Pinch salt
- Pinch pepper
- Pinch garlic powder
- 2 tbsp cream cheese

- Knob of butter
- 2 slices of bread
- 2 slices roast beef
- 1 slice onion

1 Switch on the toastie maker.

2 While it heats, put the cream cheese in a small bowl and stir in the salt, pepper and garlic powder.

3 Peel and chop a slice of onion. Shred the roast beef.

4 Spread butter on one side of each piece of bread. Spread the cream cheese mixture on the other side.

5 Place one slice of bread, butter side down, in the toastie maker. Add the roast beef and sprinkle with the chopped onion. Place the other slice of bread, butter side up, on the top.

6 Close the lid tightly and cook until the toastie is golden brown and heated through.

Half a clove of crushed garlic instead of garlic powder is fine too.

Chicken and Rocket Toastie

Ingredients

- Vegetable or sunflower oil for brushing
- 2 slices of grilled chicken breast
- 2 slices bread
- 2 tsp mayonnaise (or to taste)
- 2 tsp Dijon mustard (or to taste)
- 2 slices cheese
- A few rocket leaves

1 Use leftover cooked chicken if you have it. If not, grill the chicken breast on both sides until it is cooked through, then remove the chicken to cool and switch off the grill.

2 Brush your toastie maker with a little oil to help prevent sticking and make your toastie nice and crispy. Switch on the machine and bring it up to temperature.

3 Meanwhile, spread a thin layer of mayonnaise and mustard on each slice of bread. Cut a couple of slices of cheese, and rinse a few rocket leaves.

4 Place a slice of cheese on one piece of bread. Add the chicken and rocket, and then the other slice of cheese. Top with remaining bread.

5 Transfer your sandwich to the toastie maker. Close the lid tightly and cook until the cheese is melted and the toastie is crisp and golden brown.

Burger Toastie

Ingredients

- Vegetable or sunflower oil for brushing
- 2 slices of bread
- 1 large burger
- 2 cheese slices
- Ketchup
- 1 tomato

1 Fry or grill the burger until cooked through. Place it on a piece of kitchen roll to drain off any excess fat.

2 Brush your toastie maker with a little oil to help prevent sticking and make your toastie nice and crispy. Switch on the machine and bring up to temperature.

3 Rinse and slice the tomato. Spread some ketchup on both slices of bread. Place one slice in your toastie maker. Add a slice of cheese, with the burger on top. Add the tomato slices and the other slice of cheese. Top with the other slice of bread.

4 Close the lid tightly and cook until the cheese is melted and the toastie is crisp and golden brown.

If you prefer, substitute mayonnaise, or another burger topping of your choice, for the ketchup.

Chicken and Mustard Toastie

Ingredients

- Vegetable or sunflower oil for brushing
- 2 slices of bread
- 2 slices roast chicken
- 2 tsp Dijon mustard
- Parmesan cheese
- Salt and Pepper

1 Brush your toastie maker with a little oil to help prevent sticking and make your toastie nice and crispy. Switch on the machine and bring up to temperature.

2 Place one slice of bread in your heated toastie maker. Arrange the chicken over the top, season with salt & pepper and spread with mustard. Grate some Parmesan over the top. Cover with the remaining slice of bread.

3 Close the lid tightly and cook until the toastie is crisp and golden brown.

If you don't have Parmesan, grate some Cheddar instead, or just add a slice of cheese.

fish

toasties

Tuna and Rosemary Toastie

Ingredients

- 1 small tin tuna in olive oil
- 1 slice onion
- 1 sprig rosemary
- Black pepper

- 2 slices cheese
- 2 slices bread
- Knob of butter

1 Switch on your toastie maker to pre-heat.

2 Meanwhile, peel and finely chop a slice of onion. Open a tin of tuna and drain. Tip the tuna into a small bowl. Add the onion. Rinse the rosemary, strip off the leaves and chop them. Add them to the tuna with some black pepper, and mix. Cut two large slices of cheese.

3 Butter the bread and place one slice, butter side down, in your toastie maker. Place one slice of cheese on top, then spread on the tuna mixture. Add the second slice of cheese and top with the remaining slice of bread, butter side up.

4 Close the lid of the machine tightly and leave to cook until the toastie is crisp and golden brown.

Sardine and Tomato Toastie

Ingredients

- 1 tin sardines in BBQ sauce
- 2 slices bread
- Knob of butter
- Black pepper
- 2 slices tomato

1 Switch on your toastie maker to pre-heat.

2 Meanwhile, open a tin of sardines. Mash the fish in a small bowl with some black pepper.

3 Rinse and slice a tomato.

4 Butter the bread and place one slice, butter side down, in your toastie maker. Spread the fish on and top with tomato slices.

5 Close the lid of the machine tightly and leave to cook until the toastie is crisp and golden brown.

Sardines are oily fish that have many health benefits, including boosting your brain focus.

Easy Salmon Toastie

Ingredients

- Sunflower oil for brushing
- 2 slices bread
- 2 tsp tomato pasta sauce
- 1 small tin flaked salmon

- Black pepper
- ¼ red pepper
- 30g/1oz mature Cheddar cheese

1 Lightly brush your toastie maker with sunflower oil and switch it on to pre-heat.

2 Meanwhile, open a tin of salmon and mash in a small bowl with some black pepper to taste.

3 Rinse, core and chop the red pepper. Grate the cheese.

4 Smear the sauce on both slices of bread and then spread the salmon on top. Scatter the red pepper over it and then the cheese. Close the sandwich with the second slice of bread and transfer to the toastie machine

5 Close the lid tightly and leave to cook until the toastie is crisp and golden brown.

Any tinned fish will work with this recipe too, e.g. tuna, pilchards, sardines.

Smoked Mackerel Toastie

Ingredients

- 1 small smoked mackerel fillet, skinned and flaked
- 2 slices bread
- Knob of butter, for spreading
- 1 tsp English or mild mustard
- 1 tsp creamed horseradish or ketchup
- ½ stalk celery, finely chopped

1 Switch on your toastie maker to preheat.

2 Meanwhile, rinse and finely chop the celery. Butter the bread on one side, and smear mustard over the other side.

3 Skin and flake the fish into a bowl and mix with the horseradish and celery.

4 Place one slice of bread, butter side down in the toastie maker. Spread the mackerel mixture over it and add the other slice of bread, butter side up.

5 Close the lid of the machine tightly and cook until the toastie is crisp and golden brown.

Mackerel is a sustainabe fish you can pick up easily at any supermarket.

Smoked Trout Toastie

Ingredients

- Sunflower oil for brushing
- 50g/2oz smoked trout slices
- 2 slices of bread
- 2 tsp pesto
- 2 slices cheese
- Salt and ground black pepper

1 Lightly brush your toastie maker with sunflower oil and switch it on to pre-heat.

2 Meanwhile, cut the cheese slices.

3 Spread pesto over both slices of bread. Arrange the smoked trout on one slice. Season with salt and pepper. Add the cheese slices and cover with the remaining slice of bread, pesto side down.

4 Close the lid of the machine tightly and cook until the toastie is crisp and golden brown.

Smoked salmon also works well with this recipe, as does smoked mackerel which is usually cheaper.

Fish Finger & Baked Bean Toastie

Ingredients

- 2 slices bread
- Knob of butter
- 3 fish fingers

- 50g/2oz Cheddar cheese
- 5 tsp baked beans

1 Grill or fry the fish fingers according to the packet instructions.

2 Switch on your toastie maker to preheat.

3 Grate the cheese and butter the bread on both sides.

4 Place one slice of bread in the preheated toastie machine and layer on the cooked fish fingers, beans and cheese. Top with the remaining slice of bread.

5 Close the lid of the machine tightly and cook until the toastie is crisp and golden brown.

Baked beans are rich in protein and iron and help keep your energy levels high.

Quick & Easy Tuna Toastie

Ingredients

- Sunflower oil for brushing
- 2 slices bread
- 1 tin tuna
- Handful grated cheese

CLASSIC

1 Lightly brush your toastie maker with sunflower oil and switch it on to pre-heat.

2 Meanwhile, drain the tuna. Grate a handful of cheese and spread about a third over one slice of bread. Add half the tuna, some more cheese, and then the rest of the tuna. Top with the remaining cheese, and close the sandwich with the second slice of bread.

3 Transfer the sandwich to the toastie machine and close the lid tightly. Cook until the cheese melts and the bread is crispy and golden brown.

Tuna is a source of complete protein, providing all 10 amino acids your body needs to survive. So it helps to support brain function and maintain healthy tissue.

Chilli Tuna Toastie

Ingredients

- Sunflower oil for brushing
- ½ stalk celery
- 1 spring onion
- ½ small chilli
- 1 tin tuna
- 1 tbsp mayonnaise
- Salt
- 2 slices bread
- 2 slices Cheddar cheese

1 Lightly brush your toastie maker with sunflower oil and switch it on to pre-heat.

2 Meanwhile, rinse and finely chop the celery, spring onion and chilli (removing the seeds). Drain the tuna and mix it in a bowl with the mayonnaise, celery, spring onion and chilli. Season with salt to taste.

3 Place one slice of bread in the toastie machine. Add a slice of cheese and spread on the tuna mixture. Leave some for another day if it's too much. Top with the other slice of cheese, and the remaining bread.

4 Close the lid of the machine tightly and cook until the cheese melts and the toastie is crisp and golden brown

If you don't have spring onions, a slice of red or white onion works too.

Prawn Toastie

Ingredients

- Sunflower oil for brushing
- 2 slices white bread
- 75g/3oz cooked prawns
- 1 tbsp mayonnaise
- Dash of Tabasco sauce or pinch of chilli powder
- Salt and pepper

1 Rinse prawns in cold water. Tip them into a bowl.

2 Lightly brush your toastie maker with sunflower oil and switch it on to pre-heat.

3 Mix together the prawns, mayo, Tabasco, salt and pepper.

4 Place one slice of bread in the heated toastie maker. Spread on the prawn mixture and cover with the other slice of bread.

5 Close the lid of the machine tightly and cook until crispy and golden brown.

Try using Rose Marie sauce in place of mayo if you like.

Sandwich Paste Toastie

Ingredients

- 1 tbsp cream cheese
- Knob of butter
- 2 slices bread
- 1 tbsp mayonnaise

- ½ tomato finely chopped
- Salt & pepper
- 1 tbsp fish sandwich paste

1 Switch on your toastie maker and pre-heat.

2 Mix together the cream cheese, mayo, chopped tomato and fish paste,

3 Butter the bread. Lay one slice, butter side down, in the toastie maker. Spread the fish mixture over it and add the other slice of bread, butter side up.

4 Close the lid of the machine tightly and cook until crispy and golden brown.

Jars of fish sandwich paste are super cheap and pack a powerful punch in your toasties.

Crab Toastie

Ingredients

- 1 tin crabmeat
- 1 tbsp mayonnaise
- 1 slice of onion, chopped
- 30g/1oz Cheddar cheese

- Black pepper
- ½ tsp mustard
- 2 slices bread
- Knob of butter

1 Switch on your toastie maker and pre-heat.

2 Peel and finely chop a slice of onion. Grate the cheese.

3 Open the tin of crab, drain, and tip the crab into a small bowl. Mix in the mayonnaise, onion, cheese, mustard and pepper.

4 Butter the bread and lay one slice, butter side down, in the toastie maker. Spread the crab mixture on the bread – save some for another day if there's too much - and top with the other slice, butter side up.

5 Close the lid of the machine tightly and cook until the cheese melts and the bread is crispy and golden brown.

If you prefer, use tartar sauce instead of mayonnaise.

veggie

toasties

Cheese, Mushroom and Pepper Toastie

Ingredients

- Knob of butter
- 2 slices bread
- 1 clove garlic
- ½ tomato

- 1 mushroom
- ¼ red pepper
- 4 slices of mature cheese
- Black pepper for seasoning

1 Peel & finely chop a clove of garlic. Rinse and slice the tomato, mushroom and pepper. Cut four slices of cheese.

2 Butter the bread and place one slice, butter side down, in the toastie maker. Arrange 2 slices of cheese on top, then the tomato, mushroom and peppers. Sprinkle the garlic over the top along with a little black pepper. Top with the remaining cheese and cover with the second slice of bread.

3 Close the lid tightly and leave to cook for 3-4 minutes or until the cheese melts and the toastie becomes crispy and golden brown.

If you like, spread some peanut butter on the bread before you build your toastie.

Double Cheese and Onion Toastie

Ingredients

- 2 slices bread
- 1 slice onion
- Knob of butter
- Salt to taste
- 2 tsp mayonnaise

- Handful grated Parmesan cheese
- Handful grated mozzarella cheese
- A few leaves of parsley or oregano (if you've got any)

1 Switch on your toastie maker to preheat.

2 Rinse and chop the parsley or oregano. Peel and finely chop the onion. Grate the cheese and mix the two types together.

3 In a small bowl, mix the onion, herbs and mayonnaise. Season to taste.

4 Butter the bread and lay one slice, butter side down, in the toastie maker. Sprinkle on half the cheese. Spread the onion and mayonnaise over the top. Add the rest of the cheese and cover with the other slice of bread, butter side up.

5 Close the lid of the toastie maker tightly and leave to cook until the cheese melts and the toastie is crispy and golden brown.

Just use whatever cheese you have.

Cheese, Tomato and Basil Toastie

Ingredients

- 2 slices bread
- Knob of butter
- 1 slice Cheddar cheese
- ½ tomato
- ½ chilli
- ½ tsp dried basil
- Salt and pepper to taste

1 Switch on your toastie maker to preheat.

2 Cut a slice of cheese. Rinse the tomato and chilli. Slice the tomato. Deseed and thinly slice the chilli.

3 Butter the bread and place one slice, butter-side down, in the toastie maker. Layer one slice of cheese, one slice of tomato and a few slices of chilli on top. Sprinkle dried basil and salt and pepper to taste. Cover with the remaining slice of bread, butter-side up.

4 Close the lid of the toastie maker tightly and leave to cook until the cheese melts and the toastie is crispy and golden brown.

If you have fresh basil, use a few chopped leaves instead of dried.

Leek and Cheese Toastie

Ingredients

- 1 leek
- 2 slices tomato
- 2 slices bread

- Knob of butter
- 50g/2oz Cheddar cheese
- 2 tbsp mayonnaise

1 Switch on your toastie maker to preheat.

2 Rinse and chop the white part of the leek lengthways into thin strips. Wash and slice the tomato. Grate the cheese.

3 Butter the bread. Place one slice, butter side down, in the toastie maker. Cover with the leeks, half of the cheese, the tomato slices, then the remaining cheese.

4 Spread the mayonnaise on the unbuttered side of the other slice of bread and lay on the sandwich, butter side up.

5 Close the lid of the toastie maker tightly and leave to cook until the cheese melts and the toastie is crispy and golden brown.

Leeks are rich in vitamins A and K, and are great for all round health.

Veggie Sausage and Pepper Toastie

Ingredients

- 2 vegetarian sausages
- ½ red or yellow pepper
- Sunflower oil for brushing

- 50g/2oz cheese
- 2 slices of bread

1 Grill the sausages and pepper, turning frequently. (Brush the pepper with a little oil and some salt beforehand).

2 Brush your toastie maker with a little sunflower oil to help prevent sticking and to make your toastie nice and crisp. Switch it on to pre-heat.

3 Thinly slice the sausage. Chop half the pepper into chunks. Slice or grate the cheese.

4 Place one slice of bread in the heated toastie maker. Cover with half the cheese. Add the sausage and pepper and the rest of the cheese, then top with the other slice of bread.

5 Close the lid of the toastie maker tightly and cook until the cheese melts and the bread is crispy and golden brown.

Veggie sausages are a good source of protein.

Butternut Squash and Basil Toastie

Ingredients

- 100g/3½oz roasted butternut squash
- Handful fresh basil leaves
- Salt and pepper
- 50g/2oz cheese
- 2 slices bread
- A little sunflower oil for brushing

1 In a bowl, mash the cooked butternut squash. Chop the basil leaves and stir into the squash. Grate the cheese and add to the bowl with salt and pepper to taste.

2 Brush your toastie maker with a little sunflower oil to help prevent sticking and to make your toastie nice and crisp. Switch it on to pre-heat.

3 Spread the squash mixture onto one slice of bread and cover with the other.

4 Transfer the sandwich to the heated toastie maker. Close the lid tightly and cook until the cheese melts and the bread is crispy and golden brown.

The butternut squash is jam-packed with nutrients, including vitamin B6 which is good for the brain and nervous system.

Pepper and Spinach Toastie

Ingredients

- 2 slices bread
- Knob of butter
- 1 tomato
- 50g/2oz cheese

- 2 slices red or yellow pepper
- Handful baby spinach
- Pinch black pepper

1 Switch on your toastie maker to pre-heat.

2 Rinse and thinly slice the tomato and pepper. Wash and chop the spinach leaves. Grate the cheese.

3 Butter the bread. Put one slice, butter side down, in the toastie maker. Cover with half the cheese, and arrange the pepper, spinach and tomato on top. Sprinkle with a little black pepper and add the rest of the cheese.

Cover with the other slice of bread, butter side up.

4 Close the lid of the toastie maker tightly and cook until the cheese melts and the bread is crispy and golden brown.

Spinach is a superfood, rich in antioxidants and nutrients essential for a healthy brain and body.

Kidney Bean & Salsa Toastie

Ingredients

- ½ red or yellow pepper
- 2 tbsp tinned kidney beans
- 1-2 tsp salsa

- 2 slices bread
- Knob of butter
- 50g/2oz cheese

1 Switch on your toastie maker to pre-heat.

2 Meanwhile, tip the beans into a bowl with the salsa and mash them together. Thinly slice or grate the cheese.

3 Butter the bread and place one slice, butter side down, in the toastie maker. Arrange the cheese and mashed beans on the bread. Cover with the remaining slice of bread, butter side up.

4 Close the lid of the toastie maker tightly and cook until the cheese melts and the bread is crispy and golden brown.

If you prefer a bit more texture, leave some of the kidney beans whole while you mash the rest.

Avocado, Tomato and Pepper Toastie

Ingredients

- ½ tomato
- ½ red or yellow pepper
- ½ ripe avocado
- Knob of butter

- 2 slices of bread
- Dash of olive oil (optional)
- Black pepper

1 Switch on your toastie maker to pre-heat.

2 Meanwhile, rinse and slice the tomato and pepper. Peel, stone and slice the avocado.

3 Butter both sides of the bread. Place one slice in the toastie maker and layer on the slices of avocado, tomato & pepper and drizzle a tiny amount of olive oil over the top. Season and top with the other slice of bread.

4 Close the lid of the toastie maker tightly and cook until the bread is crispy and golden brown.

Avocados are another superfood, and high in antioxidants that are important for eye health.

Sweetcorn and Chilli Toastie

······· Ingredients ·······

- Sunflower oil for brushing
- 2 slices bread
- 1 tbsp tinned sweetcorn
- ¼ green pepper

- ½ green chilli
- 50g/2oz cheese
- Black pepper

1 Brush your toastie maker with a little sunflower oil to prevent sticking and help make your toastie nice and crisp.

2 Open a tin of sweetcorn and drain. Put a tablespoonful in a bowl. Rinse and finely chop the green pepper and the chilli (removing the seeds from the chilli). Add them to the bowl. Grate the cheese and throw that in too. Season with black pepper and mix them together.

3 Lay one slice of bread in the toastie maker. Spread on the sweetcorn mixture and cover with the other slice of bread.

4 Close the lid of the toastie maker tightly and cook until the cheese melts and the bread is crispy and golden brown.

You can use frozen sweetcorn too; just boil it for a minute or two first.

Leftover Veggie Toastie

Ingredients

- Handful of mixed, cooked vegetables (e.g., carrots, green beans, broccoli, cauliflower, or anything you have leftover)
- 1 tbsp mayonnaise
- Salt and pepper
- Knob of butter
- 2 slices bread
- ½ tomato

1 Switch on your toastie maker to pre-heat.

2 Meanwhile, mash the vegetables with the mayonnaise and season with salt and pepper. Rinse and slice the tomato.

3 Butter the bread, and place one slice in the toastie maker, butter side down. Spread the veggie mixture on the bread and top with the tomato slices. Cover with the remaining slice of bread, butter side up.

4 Close the lid of the toastie maker tightly and cook until the cheese melts and the bread is crispy and golden brown.

Use ketchup instead of mayonnaise if you prefer.

Hot Bean Toastie

Ingredients

- Sunflower oil for brushing
- ½ sweet potato, cooked
- Pinch Cayenne pepper
- 25g/1oz cheese, grated

- 1 tbsp tinned mixed beans
- A few lettuce leaves
- 2 tsp mayonnaise
- 2 slices bread

1 Brush your toastie maker with a little sunflower oil to prevent sticking and make your toastie nice and crisp. Switch it on to pre-heat.

2 Meanwhile, mash the sweet potato in a bowl with the cheese and Cayenne pepper.

3 Butter the bread, and place one slice in the toastie maker. Spread the potato mixture on the bread. Add the lettuce on top, then the beans and the mayonnaise.

Cover with the remaining slice of bread.

4 Close the lid of the toastie maker tightly and cook until the bread is crispy and golden brown.

Just drop the sweet potato if you don't have any.

Apple and Cheese Toastie

Ingredients

- 1 apple
- 1 handful of grated cheese
- 2 slices of bread
- Knob of butter
- Pinch of ground cinnamon

1 Switch on your toastie maker to pre-heat.

2 Peel , core and slice the apple. Grate the cheese.

3 Butter the bread and place one in the heated toastie maker, butter side down. Scatter half the cheese on the bread and arrange the apple slices on top. Sprinkle with cinnamon, add the rest of the cheese and cover with the other slice of bread, butter side up.

4 Close the lid of the toastie maker tightly and cook until the cheese melts and the bread is crispy and golden brown.

Cheese contains a host of vital nutrients, including calcium which is important for healthy bones and well being.

around the world toasties

Basic American Cheese Toastie

Ingredients

- 2 slices bread
- Knob of butter
- 1 white processed cheese slice
- 1 yellow processed cheese slice
- 2 tsp American mustard

1 Switch on your toastie maker to pre-heat.

2 Meanwhile, butter the bread. On the unbuttered side spread the mustard on one slice. Layer the white and yellow cheese slices. Top with the second slice of bread, butter side up.

3 Transfer the sandwich to the heated toastie maker. Close the lid tightly and leave to cook until the cheese is melted and the bread is crispy and golden brown.

Enjoy with a dollop of American sauce!

Mexican Guacamole Toastie

Ingredients

- Sunflower oil for brushing
- 2 slices white bread
- 1 tbsp guacamole
- Handful grated cheese
- Pinch chilli powder or chopped chilli

1 Brush your toastie maker with a little sunflower oil to help prevent sticking and make your toastie nice and crispy. Switch it on to pre-heat.

2 Meanwhile, grate a handful of cheese. Spread a tablespoon of guacamole on one slice of bread and top with the grated cheese and chilli.

3 Transfer the sandwich to the heated toastie maker. Close the lid tightly and leave to cook until the cheese is melted and the bread is crispy and golden brown.

Guacamole is made from avocado tomato and lime juice, so is high in vitamin C and good for your brain, energy levels and general health!

Swiss Cheese Toastie

Ingredients

- Knob of butter
- 1 garlic clove
- 2 slices bread
- 50g/2oz Emmental cheese
- 1 slice ham
- 2 cornichons sliced lengthwise

1 Switch on your toastie maker to pre-heat.

2 Soften the butter and crush a garlic clove into it, mashing to make garlic butter.

3 Cut 2 slices of cheese. Slice two cornichons lengthwise.

4 Spread the garlic butter on the bread. Place one slice, butter side down, in the toastie maker. Place 1 slice of the cheese on top, add the ham and the cornichons and the remaining cheese. Top with the second slice of bread, garlic butter side up.

5 Close the lid of the toastie machine tightly and cook until the cheese is melted and the bread is crispy and golden brown.

Use any other pickled gherkins you've got it doesn't need to be cornichons.

Curried Egg Toastie

Ingredients

- 2 eggs
- Sunflower oil for brushing
- 2 tsp mayonnaise
- 1 tsp curry powder
- Salt and pepper
- 2 slices bread

1 Hard boil the eggs (around 8 minutes). Rinse them under cold water to cool and peel off the shells. Drop the peeled eggs in a bowl.

2 Brush your toastie maker with a little sunflower oil to help prevent sticking and make your toastie nice and crispy. Switch it on to pre-heat.

3 Meanwhile, mash the eggs with a fork. Mix in the mayonnaise and curry powder. Season to taste with salt and pepper.

4 Place one slice of bread in the heated toastie maker. Spread on the egg mixture and top with the other slice of bread.

5 Close the lid of the toastie machine tightly and cook until the toastie is crispy and golden brown.

Use mild or hot curry powder – whichever you prefer.

Italian Salami and Cheese Toastie

Ingredients

- 4 slices Italian salami
- 3 slices Italian cheese
- 2 slices bread
- Knob of butter

BELLISSIMO!

1 Switch on your toastie maker to pre-heat.

2 Meanwhile, dice the salami and cheese slices, and butter the bread.

3 When the toastie maker is up to temperature, place one slice of bread, butter side down, in the machine. Evenly scatter the salami and cheese across the bread, and top with the other slice of bread, butter side up.

4 Close the lid of the toastie machine tightly and cook until the cheese is melted and the toastie is crispy and golden brown.

Provolone is a lovely Italian cheese but use whatever you have to hand.

Spicy Spanish Cheese Toastie

Ingredients

- ½ tomato
- ¼ red onion
- 50g/2oz Manchego cheese
- Pinch chilli powder
- 2 slices bread
- Knob of butter

1 Switch on your toastie maker to pre-heat.

2 Meanwhile, rinse and finely chop the tomato. Peel and finely chop the onion. Grate the cheese. Combine everything in a bowl.

3 Butter the bread. Lay one slice, butter side down, in the toastie maker. Spread on the cheese mixture and cover with the remaining slice of bread, butter side up.

4 Close the lid of the toastie machine tightly and cook until the cheese is melted and the toastie is crispy and golden brown.

If you can't get Manchego, use half Parmesan and half Cheddar – less Spanish but still tasty!

French Onion Toastie

Ingredients

- Knob of butter
- ½ tbsp olive oil
- 1 onion
- Salt and freshly cracked black pepper
- 1 tsp fresh thyme
- 2 slices French Gruyère cheese
- 2 slices bread
- Salted butter, softened

1 Heat the butter and olive oil in a frying pan. Peel and slice the onion and throw it in the pan. Cook on a low heat and sauté for about 10 minutes. Meanwhile, rinse and finely chop the thyme. Add it to the onions and season with salt and pepper. Cook for another 5 minutes. Remove from the heat and set aside.

2 Brush your toastie maker with a little sunflower oil to help prevent sticking and make your toastie nice and crisp. Switch it on to pre-heat.

3 Meanwhile, lay a slice of cheese on one slice of bread. Spread the onions over it, add the other slice of cheese and cover with the remaining slice of bread.

4 Transfer the sandwich to the heated toastie machine. Close the lid tightly and cook until the cheese is melted and the toastie is crisp and golden brown.

Peanut Butter, Jelly & Banana Toastie

Ingredients

- 2 slices good quality white bread
- Knob of butter
- 1 tbsp peanut butter

- ½ tbsp jam
- ½ banana sliced

1 Switch on your toastie maker to pre-heat.

2 Butter the bread, then turn both slices over. Spread peanut butter on the back of one slice, and the jam of your choice on the back of the other.

3 Peel and slice the banana.

4 Place one slice of bread, butter side down, in the toastie maker. Arrange the slices of banana on the top, and cover with the other slice of bread, butter side up.

5 Close the lid of the toastie maker tightly and cook until the bread is crispy and golden brown.

Try different jams for a variety of flavours!

Halloumi and Tomato Toastie

Ingredients

- **2 slices bread**
- **Knob of butter**
- **Few slices of Halloumi cheese**
- **1 fresh tomato**
- **1 tsp pesto**

1 Switch on your toastie maker to pre-heat.

2 Cut enough slices of Halloumi to cover a slice of bread. Rinse and slice the tomato.

3 Butter the bread and place one slice in the toastie maker, butter side down. Spread the pesto on the unbuttered side. Arrange the Halloumi slices on top, add the tomato slices and cover with the remaining slice of bread, butter side up.

4 Close the lid of the toastie maker tightly and cook until the cheese melts and the bread is crispy and golden brown.

Substitute mayonnaise for pesto if you like.

Indian Chutney & Cheese Toastie

Ingredients

- Sunflower oil for brushing
- 2 slices bread
- 50g/2oz cheese

- 1 medium tomato
- ¼ small red onion
- 1 tbsp mango chutney

1 Brush your toastie maker with a little sunflower oil and switch on to pre-heat.

2 Slice or grate the cheese. Rinse the tomato and slice. Peel and finely slice the onion.

3 Spread the chutney over both pieces of bread. Arrange the cheese, tomato and onion on one of them. Cover with the other piece of bread.

4 Close the lid of the toastie maker tightly and cook until the cheese melts and the bread is crispy and golden brown.

Add a little spice too if you like.

Korean Egg Toastie

Ingredients

- 2 eggs
- 1 small carrot
- 1 slice onion
- 1 tbsp sunflower oil, plus more for brushing
- 2 slices bread
- Salt and pepper
- 1 large slice cheese
- 1 slice ham
- ½ tbsp tomato ketchup

1 Crack the eggs into a bowl and whisk them.

2 Peel and finely slice the carrot & onion and add to the beaten egg.

3 Heat the oil in a small frying pan and pour in the egg mixture. Cook gently for about 2 minutes, then turn the omelette and cook for another minute. Set aside.

4 Brush your toastie maker with a little sunflower oil and switch on to pre-heat.

5 Place the cheese on one slice of bread. Add the ham, then the cooked omelette (folding it as necessary), along with the ketchup. Cover with the second slice of bread.

6 Close the lid of the toastie maker tightly and cook until the cheese melts and the bread is crispy and golden brown.

This recipe is based on Korean street food.

grilled & open toasties

Banana, Bacon and Cheese Toastie

Ingredients

- 2 slices bacon
- 1 banana
- 40g/1½oz Cheddar cheese
- Black pepper to taste
- 2 slices bread

1 Grill the bacon until crispy. Leave the grill on, and roughly chop the bacon.

2 Grate the cheese.

3 Peel the banana and mash it in bowl. Add the bacon, cheese and pepper.

4 Toast one side of each bread slice under the grill, then turn and toast the other side very slightly. Arrange the bacon and banana mixture evenly onto both slices.

5 Slide back under the grill and cook until bubbling.

Makes a great breakfast or any-time snack!

Tuna Mayonnaise Melt

Ingredients

- ½ celery stalk
- 1 slice onion
- 1 tbsp chopped parsley
- 1 tomato
- 4 slices cheese
- 1 tin tuna in brine
- 1 tbsp mayonnaise
- Salt and freshly ground black pepper
- 2 slices bread

1 Pre-heat the grill.

2 Rinse and chop half a stalk of celery, and a sprig of parsley. Peel and chop a slice of onion. Rinse and slice a tomato and cut the slices of cheese.

3 Open a tin of tuna and drain. Tip the tuna into a bowl, and mix in the mayonnaise, celery, onion and parsley. Season with salt and pepper.

4 Lightly toast the bread under the grill, then remove from the heat and spread each slice with the tuna mixture. Place one cheese slice over the tuna on each piece of bread, add tomato slices, and top with remaining cheese.

5 Slide back under the grill for 2 or 3 minutes, until cheese is melted.

You can use any bread you like, but this is particularly nice with a granary loaf.

Courgette and Tomato Toastie

Ingredients

- ½ courgettes
- 40g/1½ mozzarella cheese
- Knob of butter
- 1 pinch chilli flakes
- Salt and pepper to taste
- 2 tbsp tomato pasta sauce
- 2 slices bread

1 Preheat the grill.

2 Meanwhile, rinse the courgette and cut it into cubes. Grate the mozzarella.

3 Melt butter in a frying pan over medium heat. Fry the courgette until browned and slightly tender. Season with red chilli flakes, salt and pepper, and stir in the pasta sauce. Cook and stir until sauce is heated.

4 Toast one side of each bread slice under the grill, then turn and toast the other side very slightly. Spread the courgette mixture onto one slice of bread. Top with the mozzarella and cover with the other slice of bread. Slide under the grill and toast both sides of the sandwich.

For a thicker topping using tomato puree rather than pasta sauce.

Cheese and Chutney Toastie

Ingredients

- 100g/3½oz cheese, grated
- 1 small egg
- ½ tsp English mustard
- Salt and ground black pepper
- 2 slices bread
- 1 tbsp chutney

1 Pre-heat the grill.

2 In a bowl, stir together the cheese, egg, mustard and seasoning.

3 Spread the chutney over one slice of bread. Spread the cheese mix over the other. Place the first slice over the other, chutney side down.

4 Put the sandwich under the grill and toast until the bread is golden brown and the cheese is starting to melt. Eat immediately.

Also lovely with mango chutney!

Grilled Sausage and Cheese Toastie

Ingredients

- 2 cooked sausages
- 40g/1½oz cheese
- 2 slices bread
- Salt to taste

GREAT FOR BREAKFAST

1 Pre-heat the grill.

2 Grill the sausages until cooked through. Slice the cooked sausage, and cut the cheese into strips. Mix them together in a bowl and season with salt.

3 Toast one side of each bread slice under the grill, then turn and toast the other side very slightly.

4 Spoon the sausage mixture on top of each slice of bread and slide them under the grill until the cheese is melted and bubbling.

For a posher taste add a teaspoon of fennel seeds or for a bit of crunch try pumpkin seeds instead.

Grilled Avocado and Mushroom Toastie

Ingredients

- ½ avocado
- 50g/2oz mushrooms
- 1 tomato
- 2 slices cheese
- 2 slices bread

1 Pre-heat the grill.

2 Peel and slice the avocado. Rinse and slice the mushrooms and tomato. Cut 2 large slices of cheese.

3 Lightly toast the bread under the grill. Then cover each slice with avocado, mushrooms and tomato. Top each with a slice of cheese.

4 Slide back under the grill until the cheese melts and begins to bubble. Serve.

Mushrooms are the only fruit or vegetable source of the critical "sunshine" vitamin D, which is important for mental health.

Pear and Ham Toastie

Ingredients

- 2 slices bread
- ½ tbsp mustard
- 4 slices ham
- ½ pear
- Black pepper
- 60g/2 ½oz mozzarella cheese (or whatever cheese you've got)

1 Preheat the grill.

2 Peel and slice the pear, and grate the mozzarella.

3 Lightly toast the bread under the grill. Then spread one slice with the mustard. Layer on the ham, pear slices, a dash of pepper, and the mozzarella cheese. Top with other slice of bread.

4 Slide back under the grill and toast both sides of the sandwich until the cheese begins to melt and the bread is toasted golden brown.

Try serving with a fresh green salad.

Grilled Cheesy Mushroom Toastie

Ingredients

- 6 mushrooms
- 4 plum tomatoes, sliced
- 1 tbsp soy sauce
- Knob of butter

- 2 splashes Worcestershire sauce
- 2 slices bread
- 2 handfuls cheese

1 Pre-heat the grill.

2 Wash and finely slice the mushrooms and tomatoes. Throw the mushrooms in a microwavable bowl with the butter and soy sauce and cook in the microwave on full power for 1 min.

3 Lightly toast the bread under the grill. Smear a spoonful of the butter sauce from the cooked mushrooms onto the bread, then arrange a layer of mushrooms onto each slice of toast.

4 Add layers of cheeses, tomatoes and mushrooms, covering the toast to the edges. Finish with a layer of cheese, then drizzle Worcestershire sauce over the top.

5 Slide back under the grill and cook until the cheese bubbles and begins to brown.

For extra spice, add a chopped chilli to the mix.

Maple Syrup Bacon and Egg Toastie

Ingredients

- 2 rashers bacon
- 2 tsp maple syrup
- 2 tbsp butter, softened

- 1 large egg
- 3 slices Cheddar
- 2 slices bread

1 Pre-heat the grill.

2 Cut the cheese slices.

3 Grill the bacon rashers until they're cooked. Smear them with the maple syrup and slide them back under the grill for a minute or two (to caramelise the syrup) then set aside.

4 Fry the egg in a knob of butter, and set aside on a plate

5 On one slice of bread, layer one slice of cheese, the bacon, more cheese, the egg and the last slice of cheese. Close the sandwiches with the remaining bread.

6 Put the sandwich under the grill and toast until the bread is golden brown. Turn it and grill the other side until it is brown too and the cheese is melted.

7 Try making this with sweet brioche bread.

Simple Grilled Cheese and Tomato Toastie

Ingredients

- 1 tomato
- 2 slices of bread
- 3 slices mature Cheddar cheese
- Knob of butter

TASTY!

1 Pre-heat the grill.

2 Rinse and slice the tomato. Cut 3 slices of cheese.

3 Lightly toast one side of the bread under the grill. Turn one slice and layer on top 2 slices of cheese, tomato slices and then the remaining slice of cheese. Close the sandwiches with the remaining bread, toasted side down.

4 Slide the sandwich under the grill and toast both sides until the cheese begins to melt and the bread is golden brown.

Try sprinkling a little ground nutmeg or Cayenne pepper on the cheese as you layer the sandwich.

Guacamole and Bacon Toastie

Ingredients

- 2 slices bacon
- 2 slices bread
- 60g/2 ½ oz cheese
- 2 tbsp guacamole

◀ TRY WITH CHILLI FLAKES

1 Pre-heat the grill.

2 While it's warming, grate the cheese.

3 Grill the bacon on until it's cooked and crispy then set aside.

4 On one slice of bread, sprinkle half of the cheese, then spread on the guacamole. Add the bacon, and the remaining cheese and finally the remaining slice of bread.

5 Slide the sandwich under the grill and toast on both sides until the bread is golden brown and the cheese has melted.

For added crunch, you could crumble some tortilla chips over the bacon as you layer the sandwich.

Grilled Cheese and Pesto Toastie

Ingredients

- 2 slices bread
- 60g/2½oz cheese
- 3 tbsp pesto

RED OR GREEN PESTO

1 Pre-heat the grill.

2 While it's warming, grate the cheese. Sprinkle half of it over one slice of bread. Spread the pesto generously over the top and cover with the other slice of bread.

3 Slide the sandwich under the grill and toast both sides until the bread is golden brown and the cheese has melted.

Pesto is made from basil, olive oil, garlic, parmesan cheese and pine nuts, all healthy ingredients, and although it's high in fat, the fat is unsaturated and therefore good for you in moderation!

Grilled Chicken and Cheese Toastie

Ingredients

- 2 slices bread
- ½ tbsp mayonnaise
- 2 tbsp cream cheese
- Handful of Cheddar cheese
- 40g/1½oz cooked chicken breast
- Few drops of Tabasco

1 Pre-heat the grill.

2 While it's warming, grate the Cheddar and shred the chicken.

3 Combine the cheese, cream cheese and mayonnaise in a bowl, stirring together until the mixture is smooth.

4 In another bowl mix together the chicken and Tabasco.

5 Lightly toast one side of the bread under the grill and turn over. Spoon the cheese mixture onto one slice of bread and top with the chicken. Cover with the other slice of bread, toasted side down.

6 Slide the sandwich under the grill and toast both sides until the bread is golden brown and the cheese is melting.

7 Serve immediately while gooey and hot.

posh

toasties

Grape and Brie Toastie

Ingredients

- Sunflower oil for brushing
- Handful of red seedless grapes
- ½ avocado
- 2 slices seedy, wholegrain bread
- Wholegrain mustard
- 1 tbsp cream cheese
- A few slices Brie cheese
- Sea salt

1 Brush your toastie maker with a little sunflower oil to help prevent sticking and make your toastie nice and crispy. Switch it on to pre-heat.

2 Meanwhile, wash the grapes and halve them. Peel, de-stone and slice the avocado.

3 Spread mustard on one piece of bread, cream cheese on the other. Cover the mustardy bread with slices of Brie, then arrange the grapes and avocado slices. Sprinkle with a little sea salt and cover with the other slice of bread, cream-cheese side down.

4 Transfer the sandwich to the toastie maker. Close the lid tightly and cook until the cheese melts and the bread is crispy and golden brown.

Grapes have been called the world's healthiest food. They're packed with antioxidants and nutrients.

Cranberry and Camembert Toastie

Ingredients

- 2 slices white bread
- Knob of butter
- 60g/2oz Camembert cheese

- 1 tbsp cranberry sauce
- 1 dash balsamic vinegar

1 Switch on your toastie maker to pre-heat.

2 Meanwhile, butter the bread and slice the cheese.

3 Turn one slice of bread over and spread the Camembert evenly over the unbuttered side. Spread a thin layer of cranberry sauce over the cheese. Drizzle with a few drops of balsamic vinegar, and top with the remaining slice of bread, butter side up.

4 Transfer the sandwich to the heated toastie maker. Close the lid tightly and cook until the cheese melts and the bread is crispy and golden brown.

Brie makes a great substitute for Camembert.

Bacon, Brie and Goat's Cheese Toastie

Ingredients

- 3 rashers bacon
- 50g/2oz Brie cheese
- 50g/2oz goat's cheese
- ½ tomato sliced
- Handful of watercress
- 2 slices bread
- Knob of butter
- Salt and freshly ground black pepper

1 Grill the bacon until crisp. Break into pieces and set aside.

2 Switch on your toastie maker to pre-heat.

3 Meanwhile, slice the cheese. Rinse the tomato and watercress, and slice the tomato.

4 Butter the bread. Lay one slice, butter side down, in the toastie maker. Arrange the Brie slices on top, then the tomato, watercress, and goat's cheese. Top with the bacon pieces and season with salt and freshly ground black pepper. Cover with the remaining slice of bread, butter side up.

5 Close the lid of the toastie maker tightly and cook until the Brie melts and the bread is crispy and golden brown.

If you can't get goat's cheese, use mozzarella - though it isn't as posh!

Posh Chocolate Toastie

Ingredients

- 60ml/2floz evaporated milk
- 40g/1½oz dark chocolate, finely chopped
- Knob of butter
- 2 slices thin whole-wheat or white sandwich bread
- ½ tbsp dark or milk chocolate chips
- ½ tbsp chopped hazelnuts

1 First, finely chop the dark chocolate. Heat the evaporated milk in a small pan until just boiling. Add the chocolate, let it stand for one minute, and then whisk until smooth. Let cool slightly.

2 Switch on your toastie maker to pre-heat.

3 Meanwhile, butter the bread. When the toastie machine is up to temperature, place one slice in it, butter side down. Spread the chocolate mixture over the bread, almost but not quite to the edges. Sprinkle on the chocolate chips and nuts. Cover with the remaining slice of bread, butter side up.

4 Close the lid of the toastie maker tightly and cook until the toast is golden and the chocolate barely melted.

Steak and Cream Cheese Toastie

Ingredients

- 50g/2oz steak
- 30g/1oz mushrooms, sliced
- ½ garlic clove

- 1 tbsp cream cheese
- Freshly ground black pepper
- 2 Slices of thick bread

1 Grill or fry the steak as you like it, along with the sliced mushrooms.

2 Switch on your toastie maker to pre-heat.

3 Meanwhile, crush the garlic, and thinly slice the steak. Mix the cream cheese in a bowl with some black pepper and the garlic.

4 Butter the bread and place one slice, butter side down, in the toastie maker. Cover with the steak slices and mushrooms. Top with the cream cheese and cover with the remaining slice of bread, butter side up.

5 Close the lid of the toastie maker tightly and cook until the toast is crispy and golden brown.

If you don't have cream cheese, you can use a slice or two of hard cheese instead.

Creamy Crab Toastie

Ingredients

- Sunflower oil for brushing
- 1 tomato
- 125g/4oz fresh crabmeat
- ½ tbsp mayonnaise
- ½ tbsp soured cream
- 2 spring onions
- Salt and freshly ground black pepper
- 2 slices bread
- 2 tbsp grated Parmesan cheese

1 Rinse and slice the tomatoes & spring onions.

2 Brush your toastie maker with a little sunflower oil to help prevent sticking and make your toastie nice and crispy. Switch it on to pre-heat.

3 Meanwhile, in a medium bowl, gently mix the crabmeat, mayonnaise, soured cream and spring onions. Season with salt and pepper.

4 Place one slice of bread in the toastie maker. Arrange the slices of tomato on top, followed by the crabmeat mixture. Sprinkle the Parmesan cheese evenly over the top. Cover with the remaining slice of bread.

5 Close the lid of the toastie maker tightly and cook until the toast is crispy and golden brown.

Serve with a leafy green salad.

Smoked Salmon and Cream Cheese Toastie

Ingredients

- 2 slices bread
- 2 tbsp soft full fat cheese
- 2-3 slices smoked salmon
- Handful fresh dill
- Lemon wedges and lemon juice

1 Brush your toastie maker with a little sunflower oil to help prevent sticking and make your toastie nice and crispy. Switch it on to pre-heat.

2 Meanwhile, rinse and roughly chop the dill.

3 Lay one slice of bread in the heated toastie maker. Spread the soft cheese over it and season with salt and pepper. Arrange the salmon slices on top and sprinkle with the dill. Squeeze a dash of lemon juice over the top. Spread the remaining slice of bread with the rest of the soft cheese and place, cheesy side down, to close the sandwich.

4 Close the lid of the toastie maker tightly and cook until the toast is crispy and golden brown.

Smoked and unsmoked, salmon is one of the oily fish highest in omega 3 - serious brain food!

sweet
toasties

Chocolate, Strawberry & Banana Toastie

Ingredients

- 2 slices bread
- Knob of butter
- 1 tbsp chocolate hazelnut spread

- 2 strawberries
- ½ banana

1 Switch on your toastie maker and bring up to temperature.

2 Meanwhile, rinse the strawberries and remove the green tops. Peel and slice half a banana.

3 Butter both slices of bread on one side, and cover the other sides in chocolate spread. Place one slice, butter side down, in the heated toastie maker. Layer on the slices of strawberry and banana, and close with the other slice of bread, butter side up.

4 Close the lid tightly and cook until the bread is crispy and golden brown.

Strawberries are packed with vitamin C to help keep your brain focused.

Wicked Sweet Toastie

Ingredients

- 2 slices of bread
- Knob of butter
- 1 chocolate bar of your choosing
- 1 handful marshmallows

← GREAT WITH A SNICKERS

1 Switch on your toastie maker and bring it up to temperature.

2 Meanwhile, break the chocolate into squares or chunks. Butter the bread.

3 Place one slice of bread, butter side down, onto the heated toastie maker. Break up about 4-5 squares of chocolate onto the bread. Add a few marshmallows, but not so many that they'll spill out of the sandwich when it's shut in the machine. Top with the second slice of bread, butter side up.

4 Close the lid tightly and cook until the bread is crispy and golden brown.

Be careful as you lift it out, making sure not to get burned by drips of boiling chocolate or marshmallow.

Spiced Banana & Peanut Butter Toastie

Ingredients

- **2 slices bread**
- **Knob of butter**
- **2 tbsp crunchy peanut butter**
- **1 banana**

- **½ tsp ground cinnamon**
- **Pinch ground nutmeg**
- **Pinch all spice**
- **Pinch ground cloves**

1 Switch on your toastie maker and bring it up to temperature.

2 Meanwhile, butter the bread on one side and spread peanut butter on the other side of one of the pieces.

3 Place one slice of bread, butter side down, in the toastie maker. Peel the banana, cut it in half length-wise, and place it on top. Sprinkle on the cinnamon, nutmeg, all spice and cloves. Top with the second slice of bread, butter side up.

4 Close the lid tightly and cook until the bread is crispy and golden brown.

Peanut butter is high in protein and helps keep up your energy levels.

Cherry Cheesecake Toastie

Ingredients

- 2 slices bread
- Knob of butter
- 2 tbsp cream cheese
- 2 tbsp tinned cherry filling

TRY WITH WHIPPED CREAM

1 Switch on your toastie maker and bring it up to temperature.

2 Meanwhile, butter the bread on one side. When the machine is heated, place one slice in it, butter side down.

3 Layer on the cream cheese and cherry filling. Top with the second slice of bread, butter side up.

4 Close the lid tightly and cook until the bread is crispy and golden brown. Sprinkle with icing sugar and enjoy.

Try with brioche or other sweet bread.

Peanut Butter, Chocolate & Banana Toastie

Ingredients

- 2 slices bread
- Knob of butter
- 2 tbsp peanut butter

- ½ banana
- 3 squares of a chocolate bar
- Sprinkling of sugar

1 Switch on your toastie maker and bring it up to temperature.

2 Butter the bread one side and spread peanut butter on the other. Break your chocolate bar into squares or chunks.

3 Place one slice of bread, butter side down, in the toastie maker. Add the chocolate. Peel and slice half a banana and add that. Top with the other slice of bread, butter side up.

4 Close the lid tightly and cook until the bread is crispy and golden brown. Sprinkle with icing sugar and enjoy.

You could use chocolate spread instead of a chocolate bar.

Blueberry & Cream Cheese Toastie

Ingredients

- 1 tbsp cream cheese
- 2 tsp icing sugar, plus more for dusting
- ½ tsp grated lemon zest
- 2 slices white bread

- Knob of butter
- 1 tbsp blueberry jam (or whatever jam you have)

1 Grate a little zest from a fresh lemon.

2 Switch on your toastie maker and bring it up to temperature.

3 In a small bowl, mix the cream cheese, icing sugar and lemon zest.

4 Butter the bread on one side, and spread blueberry jam on the other.

5 Place one slice in the toastie maker, butter side down. Spoon the cheese mixture onto the centre, and top with the other slice of bread, butter side up.

6 Close the lid tightly and cook until the bread is crispy and golden brown. Sprinkle with a little more icing sugar and enjoy.

Delicious with a dollop of vanilla ice cream!

French Strawberry Toastie

Ingredients

- 4 strawberries
- A little sunflower oil for brushing
- 2 slices bread
- 1 tbsp cream cheese
- 1 egg
- Splash of milk
- Sprinkling of icing sugar

1 Rinse the strawberries and remove the green tops before slicing them.

2 Brush your toastie maker with a little sunflower oil to help prevent sticking. Switch it on and bring up to temperature.

3 Meanwhile, whisk the egg in a bowl, with a splash of milk, then transfer to a shallow container.

4 Spread cream cheese on both sides of the bread. Make a sandwich with the sliced strawberries arranged between the bread slices. Then dip the whole sandwich into the egg mixture, so it's coated on both sides.

5 Place in the pre-heated toastie maker, close the lid tightly and cook until the bread is crispy and golden.

6 When they're ready, sprinkle them with icing sugar.

Cream Egg Toastie

Ingredients

- 2 slices bread
- Knob of butter
- 1 cream egg

UNBEATABLE!

1 Switch on your toastie maker and bring up to temperature.

2 Unwrap the cream egg and soften it in the microwave for a few seconds.

3 Butter the bread and place one slice, butter side down, in the pre-heated toastie maker. Break up the cream egg and squash it on to the bread. Add the other slice, butter side up.

4 Close the lid tightly and cook until the bread is crispy and golden brown.

Classic nutritious student food!!

Brie and Honey Toastie

Ingredients

- 2 slices bread
- Knob of butter
- 50g/2oz Brie cheese, sliced about half a centimetre thick
- 1 tbsp honey

SWEET & SAVOURY

1 Switch on your toastie maker and bring up to temperature.

2 Meanwhile, cut enough slices of Brie to cover one bread slice. Butter the bread and lay one side in your pre-heated toastie maker.

3 Arrange the Brie slices on top, and add the honey. Cover with the remaining slice of bread, butter side up.

4 Close the lid tightly and cook until the bread is pale golden brown.

Honey helps the body absorb calcium and so can help boost memory and brain power as well as athletic performance.

Apple, Cinnamon & Raisin Toastie

Ingredients

- Sunflower oil for brushing
- ½ apple
- 2 slices bread
- 1 tsp icing sugar
- Pinch ground cinnamon
- Small handful raisins

1 Brush your toastie maker with a little sunflower oil to help prevent sticking and make your toastie nice and crispy. Switch it on to pre-heat.

2 Meanwhile, wash the apple, peel and core it and cut one half into thin slices. Arrange the apple over one slice of bread. Sprinkle icing sugar and a generous pinch of cinnamon over the top. Scatter over a few raisins then cover with the other slice of bread.

3 Transfer the sandwich to the toastie maker. Close the lid tightly and cook until the bread is crispy and golden brown.

Apples have a high vitamin C content, and help to focus the brain and keep you healthy.

Blackberry & White Chocolate Toastie

Ingredients

- 2 slices bread
- Knob of butter
- 1 large marshmallow
- 25g/1oz white chocolate, from a bar
- 4 ripe blackberries

1 Switch on your toastie maker to pre-heat.

2 Rinse the blackberries, then lightly mash them with a fork to break them up. Break the chocolate into small pieces.

3 Butter the bread and lay one slice in the toastie machine, butter side down. Spread the squashed blackberries on the bread, then scatter the chocolate pieces and add the marshmallow in the middle. Squash it down with the other slice of bread, butter side up.

4 Close the lid of the toastie maker tightly and cook until the bread is crispy and golden brown.

Recent studies have shown blackberries to be good for brain health.

Other COOKNATION TITLES

If you enjoyed 'Student Toasties' we'd really appreciate your feedback. Reviews help others decide if this is the right book for them so a moment of your time would be appreciated.

Thank you.

You may also enjoy...

The *Skinny* Slow Cooker Student Recipe Book
Delicious, Simple, Low Calorie, Low Budget, Slow Cooker Meals For Hungry Students. All Under 300, 400 & 500 Calories

Browse our catalogue by searching under 'CookNation' on **Amazon** or visit **www.cooknationbooks.com** and **www.bellmackenzie.com**

Printed in Great Britain
by Amazon